B$G TALK

21 WAYS TO SECURE THE BAG

YOULOVEARICA

Bag Talk: 21 Tips to Secure the Bag: Arica Scott

First Printing
ISBN 978-1-943284-55-9 (pbk.)
ISBN 978-1-943284-57-3 (ebk)

A2Z Books Publishing Lithonia, GA 30058 www.A2ZBookspublishing.net
Manufactured in the United States of America A2Z Books Publishing has allowed this work to remain exactly as the author intended, verbatim.

Introduction

I started my very first business at the age of 15. I was sitting on bed scrolling through "the gram" after just recently getting cut from the varsity tennis tryouts, not really sure what I was going to do with my life because tennis was my life. I wasn't sure what was next; I knew I couldn't get a job because I couldn't even picture myself working for someone else. My parents owned their own businesses, so working for yourself was all I knew. So I kept scrolling through insta until I saw a post of a girl's lip gloss collection and that's when it hit me, I was going to start a lip gloss line.

My first business was my cosmetic line; So Glossy Me Cosmetics, starting with the So Glossy glosses and the So Glossy gear. Flipping the money I made off of the glosses and the gear, I am now working on EYEZ by So Glossy, adding lashes and eyeshadow to the So Glossy Collection.

Of course, building my brand didn't happen overnight, but I knew that for it to grow, I was going to have to put tons of work into it. Sis, I also knew that the lifestyle I wanted was expensive, and that wasn't going to come overnight. My mom was the person who helped me start my brand (and Mr. Thomas, my economics teacher, he is a real one), but if I didn't have her I wouldn't have been able to start my business due to the lack of resources there are to teach young entrepreneurs. I decided that I would create a book that would help young people become a successful boss and most importantly, learn how to secure the bag. PERIOD.

BAG TIP #1:

BAG TIP #1 is identifying the mission and vision of your brand. Ask yourself: "What do I really want to accomplish with my business?" This will help you visualize what industry you see your business falling under and overall, what type of business you will be starting. Realizing the different subjects and topics you are interested in will help cultivate your business and the industry it will reside in.

For example, if you are into:

- **The overall topic of economics: supply and demand, goods, and services, the industry you would probably want to look into would be the stock industry.**
- **Hair, eyelash extensions, nail tech, or beauty service, then your business would fall into the beauty industry.**
- **Real estate would be a great industry if you are a contractor, you sell homes or similar services.**

Of course, there are many other industries out there that are suitable for your business. Once you have found your industry, now it's time to put together pieces of your business, finalizing what your business will be.

LISTEN, it is crucial to be in an industry that you ACTUALLY enjoy. Why would I start a business in the tech industry if I'm not passionate about the tech industry? Making sure that you have a passion in the industry you choose helps you in the long run, making you work harder and having a strong belief that the work will pay off. Also, you would never get tired of working because you're enjoying it. If you have more knowledge in your industry and are aware of the problems it comes with, your business will be easier to market.

For example, I always loved lip gloss and cosmetics. I noticed that there are tons of sticky lip glosses that aren't suitable for wind. Some leave residue on the lips while others need to be applied repeatedly. I created a lip gloss that is vegan, non-sticky, and lasts for several hours without having residue on your lips. Being aware of specific problems experienced by users made it easier for me to market my products.

Think about how your business would sell better and what makes it stand out.

Bag Talk Notes

BAG TIP #2

BAG TIP #2 is to research your industry. This is one of the most important tips in the book, and without researching your industry, you are placing your business into a lot of danger. Figuring out more information about your industry will allow you to create a business while being aware of different scenarios your business could come with. Also, gaining more knowledge will help you when you have certain encounters with clients.

When researching, make sure you use websites such as **Google Scholar, Stanford Business,** and **Good Trends** to help you find in-depth information about your business.

Certain things you would want to research about your industry would be:

- **How much money does your industry make in your location and the local states around your area yearly?**
- **What brands are dominating your industry the most, and how were those brands started?**
- **Where is the best location to get your product from? (If selling a product)**

Information I looked for while starting my business:
- **Top/leading cosmetic companies**
- **Animal cruelty products**
- **Vegan products**
- **Top beauty industry locations**

Make sure you write down and keep your notes in a journal or a google document. It is key to go back and review the information you found about your industry because there may be certain situations where you need to review your notes ASAP.

It is also crucial to go out and educate yourself about your business instead of jumping out and starting your business without really knowing anything. Knowing more about your business makes it appear more professional, and when you know less, your business will look a little messy.

<u>Bag Talk Notes</u>

BAG TIP #3

BAG TIP #3 is creating your business logo. Your logo should be a visual representation of your business or a symbol/object that best represents your business. It is imperative to have an attractive logo because it's the identity of your business. Also, your logo, along with your products, are what appears in your clients' mind when they think of you.

For example:

- **When thinking about a painting company, the first thing that appears in my mind is Sherwin Williams logo with the paint.**
- **When I think of fast food, McDonalds "M" is what instantly comes into my mind.**

Overall, your logo is crucial because it is how your clients perceive your business. When creating a logo, it is essential to take note of the key things:

- Business colors
- Interesting font
- Overall message of your business

When creating your logo, it is important to think about the future and how your business will be perceived and viewed by the public. I would suggest that you should not use profanity or anything explicit because you do not want to further yourself from possible clientele. So when creating your brand, you would want to ask yourself the questions:

- How will the public view my brand?
- Does my logo describe the overall message of my brand?
- Is my logo approaching the clientele or market I am trying to reach?

If you answered these questions with "yes," then it is also crucial to allow someone else to preview your logo to see if they can answer the questions with "yes," just to get an idea of how others will view your brand. If the person you asks agree that your logo is reasonable and most importantly, you believe in it, then you have created the perfect logo for your brand.

Bag Talk Notes

_____

_____

_____

_____

_____

_____

_____

_____

_____

_____

BAG TIP #4

BAG TIP #4 is getting your LLC paperwork together. LLC is a license that prevents you from certain situations with the companies you work with or get involved with. Getting your LLC is different for each industry, so it is important to research what it takes to get your LLC in the sector you chose. Getting the LLC for your business isn't necessarily a short process to make (corporation, LLC)

I know you are probably asking yourself what exactly is an LLC. An LLC means, limited liability companies, meaning that you will not be responsible or affected by company issues that involve debt and certain liabilities involving other brands also.

Many people get their companies registered as LLC's because it will protect their personal liabilities for certain situations involving their business liabilities.

For example: if something was to go wrong with a client you provided a service for and they wanted to take you to court, your business liabilities would be affected but not your personal liabilities.

<u>Bag Talk Notes</u>

BAG TIP #5

BAG TIP #5 is all about the money honey, identifying the pricing of the product you are selling. This is a big step in your business process because it will help to determine how you create your income. Before randomly pricing your products, there are a few areas you would like to look into. This helps create the perfect price for your products and a price that is generally good for your business.

When running a business, you want to make sure that you are constantly growing and you are bringing in money. If your business isn't bringing in money, your business isn't making sense.

Write down business expenses

When starting your business, the first thing you need to do is to write down everything – write down business card expenses, website price, etc. Knowing all of your expenses is essential because the goal is to make enough money to the point where you know longer have to pay for such expenses from your pocket, but from the income you get from your business – so, your company pays for itself.

TO MAKE A BAG, YOU HAVE TO SPEND A BAG

Of course, when starting a business, you are most definitely going to put money into it. So you want to keep up with how much money you spend each time.

Generally, once you have all the information in front of you, it will help you create a reasonable price for your product. It is important to make sure that your pricing is fair and equally crucial for your pricing to be "reasonable for YOUR BUSINESS." Create your product pricing around how much it takes to make your product.

For example, if I spend a wholesale amount of $1.50 for eyelashes purchased in bulk and sell it for $15.00-$20.00 your gross income will be $15.00 - $1.50 (expense) = $13.50-18.5 as your overall net profit.

While creating your pricing, it is important to look at the pricing of other products that are similar to yours in your industry.

Lastly, believe in your business. Do not sell your products cheap simply because you are just starting your business. Selling with low pricing isn't going to get you anywhere. Compare your price with other businesses, and if everyone else has a higher price, INCREASE YOURS, just make sure it makes sense. Do not sell your product for $5 if it is worth $10, and do not sell your product for $10 if it is worth $15.

Bag Talk Notes

BAG TALK

BAG TIP #6

BAG TIP #6 is mapping out your business colors. Business colors are the colors that will represent your brand, from your logo to your website, and most importantly, your packaging. How you package your products is how your clients will remember you; it is a part of your business identity just like your logo.

Having nice business colors helps to create lovely visuals for your brand. When people see your colors, they are likely going to think about your brand. My business colors are black and pink. My business colors are included in my packaging, websites, and the emails I send. I package my products into pink holographic bubble wraps (which is about to change soon:)), the backgrounds of the emails that I send are pink, and my website borders are pink as well.

When choosing your business color, you want to think about the colors in your logo. Incorporate your logo colors into your business colors. Also, if the product you are selling has a unique color, you could incorporate those colors into your business colors.

Bag Talk Notes

BAG TIP #7

BAG TIP #7 is creating your packaging. The way you package your products is crucial since it is how your clients will receive their products. In this case, it is important to make sure that the packaging of your products looks professional and clean. If you have a messy packaging, then that is how your brand is going to appear to clients, which results in the loss of your clientele. Every time I package an order for a client, I take my time. I make sure everything looks extremely important, professional, and clean with no marks at all.

When creating the perfect packaging, these are key to consider:
- **Labels**
- **Boxes**
- **Envelopes**
- **Returning labels**

When I package my products, I use pink holographic bubble envelopes (which is about to change soon;)) that I ordered in bulk online. Not only were the envelopes extremely affordable, but the packaging also looked very professional and stood out. I also add stickers and mirrors into my packaging so clients could look forward to receiving the products. Having good packaging also pulls people into ordering more from you.

Bag Talk Notes

BAG TIP #8

BAG TIP #8 is identifying and realizing your peeps. Your peeps will comprise a group of people who share the same interests, characteristics, etc. In business, your peeps are also called your target market. Your target market is one of the biggest factors that can determine how profitable your business will be. Everything you do revolves around your target market. Knowing who makes up your target market allows you to create and add products to your business that will sell because those products are what attracts your target market.

Your peeps (target market) consists of people who:
- Have similar characteristics
- Have similar needs
- Have similar professions
- Are located in the same locations
- Most importantly, have similar demographics

When you identify your target market, it will help you realize what your audience are into, making it easier to figure out what products to sell. Also, when you are marketing, you will know the exact group of people to market and reach out to. Knowing your target market gives you a visual of who will purchase from you and who will not because everyone isn't a part of your target market. Someone people are definitely not going to be into what you are selling, and that's ok. What truly matters right now are those who are part of your target market.

To identify your target market, it is important that you answer these questions:
- Who am I selling to? Male or female.
- What are the races of my clientele?
- Where are my clients located?
- What is the disposable income of my clients?

After answering these questions, be sure that you're able to prove how these questions are correct.

Bag Talk Notes

BAG TIP #9

BAG TIP #9 is creating your website. Your website is basically your overall store; it will be where clients will come and purchase your products or look at the services that you are providing. When creating your website, you would want to make sure that everything your business offers is displayed on your website.

When creating a website, it is essential to have:

- About Page
  - An "about page" explains what your overall business is. An about page may also include who the creator of the business is, where the business is based, and how the business was founded. An about page is the overall back story of the business.
- FAQ Page
  - A "FAQ page" displays the answers to the common questions that your customers will ask you. For example, a FAQ page would mention how your service is provided, what is in your product if selling one, and other frequently asked questions that would be commonly asked regarding what you are providing.
- Contact Page
  - A "contact page" simply lets your clients know how they could reach you if they have problems; if they need answers to questions that aren't on the FAQ page, or allows business-related companies to reach out to you. Your "contact page" would have your phone number, fax number (if you have one), email, and location.
- Terms of use
  - A "terms of use" is a page that is part of your website which explains the terms or conditions of using your product or service.
- Privacy Policy
  - A "private policy" page states legally how your business will protect all of your clients and information given to you only.

These are the pages you should add to your website and are key, especially when you encounter certain situations with clients and other business situations.

<u>Bag Talk Notes</u>

BAG TIP #10

BAG TIP #10 is finding an email system that fits well for you. Email systems help you to cultivate your clients' emails so that you can keep in touch with them. Email system companies are all different, so it is important to choose a company that is fit for you. When you have an email system, it allows you to send emails out to your clients whenever you have new deals

Email system companies:
- Mailmunch
- Mailjet
- SendiBlue
- Constant Contract
- Convertkit

I recommend using an email system from your website because it makes it easier when you are ready to send emails out to your clients. To create an email system, it is important to have an email pop up on your website. An email pop up could also allow clients to place their phone number and sometimes even their social media names so you could stay in contact with them. When your clients subscribe to the lists, your website email system will automatically put all of your clients into a subscriber list, allowing you to keep in contact with costumers.

Having an email list makes it easier to stay in contact with clients and allows you to send emails to your clients when you are having events, sales, specials, etc.

Bag Talk Notes

BAG TIP #11

BAG TIP #11 is identifying your plugs and connections. Your plugs are basically your resources and the places you will supply with your products. When you figure out your industry and what you want to sell, you would need to know where to get your resources. Your plug will supply you with the resources you need for your business. In reality, your plug is your manufacturer or where you buy your products in bulk (wholesale). For example: nowadays, people love to sell supplier information, so that can be your plug. It doesn't matter whether you are in the beauty industry or construction industry; every business owner needs a plug.

Your plug gives you access to:
- Suppliers that could provide you with your product
- Marketing
- Private labeling
- Techniques for becoming a boss

THIS BOOK IS EVEN A PLUG.

- If you are creating an eyelash company, then you would need to know where to receive mink lashes or different lash styles.
- If you want to become a stylist or a provider of hair service, then you would need to know where to get your shampoo, hair, etc.

How do you find your plugs?

Like I said earlier, nowadays, you can find resources on Instagram where people sell vendors for different things like lashes, nails, etc. It is important to find different vendors for different products. I recommend not having the same vendor for everything because you may never know what could happen to the vendor, resulting in you losing all of your products. I suggest that you shouldn't be afraid of asking other people about their vendors or where to find vendors. ASKING QUESTIONS CREATE A BIGGER BOSS.

Vendors: www.alilbaba.com

Bag Talk Notes

BAG TIP #12

BAG TIP #12 is controlling your quality control. Quality control is the control of the amount of product you put out vs. the amount of those products that sell. Managing your quality is very important because you would never want to have TOO MUCH of a product. Having TOO MUCH of a product also results in the loss of money. When you have too much of a product, it means that you ordered more products than you actually needed, leaving you left with a lot of products that you aren't going to need.

How exactly do you know the right amount of products that you need?

It is crucial to start with a reasonable number of products that you feel you could possibly sell. For example, if you are going to sell lashes and you already know about 60+ people who are interested in purchasing your product, then a reasonable quality control would be 100 or 200. When purchasing from some vendors, they require the specific number that you want to buy from them, so it is important to choose the right vendor that has a reasonable price for you.

When having too much of a product isn't a route that you would want to go in your business, then dropshipping is a better option. Also, if you feel as if you are going to have a lot of product sitting around your house or office, then it is best for you to choose the dropshipping route.

<u>Bag Talk Notes</u>

BAG TIP #13

BAG TIP #13 is creating your marketing strategy. Your market strategy is how you will get your brand discovered more. Some examples of a marketing strategy are Instagram ads, promotions, Instagram models, etc. Your market strategy is fundamental, and as things are constantly changing, it is important to have different marketing strategies that are up-to-date and a strategy that people would actually interact with.

There are a million ways to market, but it should all revolve around the goals you have for your brand and the direction you see your brand going towards in the future. When creating a marketing plan, it is important to look at the time, location, and demographics of your clientele.

Different ways of marketing are through:
- Commercials (TV, Snapchat)
- Interviews
- Adds
- Social media
- Influencers
- Emails
- Giveaway/Contests

There are a thousand other ways you could market, but this is just to name a few. To create your marketing plan, you would need to know what social media networks your clientele is on the most. For my business, the majority of my clients are on Facebook and Instagram. But it is crucial to also market on social media pages to gain attention from different crowds.

<u>Bag Talk Notes</u>

_____

_____

_____

_____

_____

_____

_____

_____

_____

_____

BAG TIP #14

BAG TIP #14 is having your gang together. Your gang will be a team of people who will support, help, and provide for you while starting your business and building your brand. It is important to have your gang together because they will help you with the support and the growth of your business.

Every good businesswoman or man has a team behind them.

Things your gang could help you with:
- Business advice
- Support
- marketing/branding
- Contacting clients
- And other things that you need to run your business

You could hire a team to help you when you start your business, but I recommend that you use some trustworthy people that you know when starting because it enables you to save money. It is essential to look at different brand teams because of the different offers each team has.

Bag Talk Notes

_____

_____

_____

_____

_____

_____

_____

_____

_____

_____

BAG TIP #15

BAG TIP #15 is creating your business' social media accounts. It is a necessity to be on social media when you have a business, and if you aren't, then you are making a huge mistake. Most companies nowadays are branding themselves on social media due to the number of people who are always on social media and their phones. Having your business on social media is crucial because you know for sure that someone is going to discover your business regardless. Period.

Social media companies for marketing your business:
- Instagram
- Facebook
- Twitter
- Snapchat
- Tumblr

I suggest that you choose a social media platform that is best for your company. For example, if you are starting a clothing line, I feel like Instagram would be a necessity for your business since people are always searching for new clothing companies on Instagram and also because clothes are always being promoted on Instagram by influencers.

Though using social media influencers is an option for promoting your business, I suggest that YOU be the promoter for your brand. It is important that you should already be promoting your brand before anyone else starts promoting for you. Believe it or not, it doesn't really matter how many followers you have; if people see you promoting a product that they like, it will bring attention to them and others.

For example:

If you only have 500 followers on Instagram and you are constantly branding yourself by posting your product and reaching out to others, then you will attract more people to your social media pages and possibly future clientele.

<u>Bag Talk Notes</u>

BAG TIP #16

BAG TAP #16 is creating a payment service for your clientele. It is crucial to offer different payment services for your clients because people have different payment methods. For example, I accept payments with PayPal, Cashapp, and Square (when I appear at an event), and just the simple credit card.

When checking out on your website, it is crucial that your website checkout offers:

- PayPal
  - PayPal is a necessity you need to have as an option when a client is checking out on your online store or just simply purchasing your product from your store. Many people use PayPal as an option to pay for things, especially online, so it is key to have that as an option, especially if you have an online business or store.
- Cashapp
  - Not many people use Cashapp as a payment service, but I think it is great, especially if you are a young entrepreneur. Nowadays, everyone has cash app – young or old. But cash app is great for young people who do not have PayPal or credits cards. I highly recommend using Cashapp or other similar brands, including brands like Venmo or Square.
- Paying with a regular card
- Square
  - If you are providing a service or vending at events, I highly recommend that you use Square. Square allows you to use a small device that you plug into your phone to swipe cards and allow clients to pay for their product using debit or credit cards. Square also provides other devices that allow you to set up your business in a store format, etc.

<u>Bag Talk Notes</u>

_____

_____

_____

_____

_____

_____

_____

_____

_____

_____

BAG TIP #17

BAG TIP #17 is figuring out the location of your clients. Finding out the locations of your clientele is essential because it gives you direct places to market and places where your business could hold future events. My top locations are Atlanta, Raleigh, and California. Now that I know that those are the places that my clientele is coming from, I market directly to those locations. Once your business becomes popular in those locations, you could then expand to other locations around your main locations.

For example:

Since Georgia and North Carolina are my top locations, I would then expand my brand to Virginia, South Carolina, and Florida.

Once you realize where your business is booming at, it will help you know the next place that is best for your business to grow. Sooner or later, you will have at least five states that are familiar with your business.

It is also important to find out where your social media followers are located. You could see this on the insights of your Instagram only if your Instagram account was activated as a business account. Learning where your followers are located will also help you with your marketing. It will be easier for you to market because you will know where you need your ads to appear.

<u>Bag Talk Notes</u>

BAG TIP #18

BAG TIP #18 DROPSHIPPING! Dropshipping is when you send your product to a company, and they ship out your product directly to your client on your behalf, instead of you doing it yourself. Normally, your supplier would ship the item for you, but some companies specialize in dropshipping. Though drop shipping is a good method, there are certainly some pros and cons you need to review before choosing to go that route with your business.

THE PROS OF DROP SHIPPING:

- You will not have to deal with having a large inventory of products sitting in your office or at home. Instead, your product will be with the company that is doing the drop shipping for you.

- You would not have to spend money on the necessities it takes to ship out your product. When using drop shipping, you would not have to pay for packaging, labels, and shipping charges.

THE CONS OF DROP SHIPPING:

- You no longer have control of how your clients will receive their products. When using drop shipping, you will not be able to see if your product is being shipped out with the same level of care you would put into the shipping process.
- If a client has a problem with their product being shipped to them, it would be hard for you to know what happened in the situation involving the order they made. You will not know if they received their product or not because you didn't ship it.
- When using drop shipping, it lowers the standards of your customer service. Like I said before, you will have no control over the care for your product, and this results in problems like the delivery of poor quality products to your customers.

Bag Talk Notes

BAG TIP #19

BAG TIP #19 would be about having quality control over your items. Quality control is when you have control over the quality of your products or the services you are providing to your clients. Quality control helps you create good quality and management of your products that you are selling. It also prevents you from making silly mistakes and allows your business to appear more organized. Here are four types of quality controls that are key when you are starting your business.

- Process Control
  o Process control describes the process of creating your products. When creating your products, you would want to make sure that everything in the process goes smooth and in order. Overall, you want to make sure that everything in the process of making your product is working correctly and the process is going just the way it's supposed to be.

- Product analysis
  o When your product is ready, it is equally important to look at your product and to double-check if there are any problems. This will help you correct simple mistakes you made during the process of making them. An example of mistakes that could be found during product analysis is the tarring of packaging, small scratches, and marks.

- Cost control
  o Analyzing the cost of your products is very important. Cost control helps you realize how much you spend on making and creating your product.

- Checklists
  o Checklists are a big factor of quality control, allowing you to review your product and your packaging. This will help ensure that everything is in the right place and that the product is in the correct state which it is supposed to be in.

<u>Bag Talk Notes</u>

_____

_____

_____

_____

_____

_____

_____

_____

_____

_____

BAG TIP #20

BAG TIP #20 would be to set the goals you would want to make for your business. For example, when I first started my business, my goal was to sell at least five glosses each week. Then I slowly expanded my goal. When starting your business, it is important to identify the goals you would want to reach each week and month. Also, it's key to make sure that your goal is reasonable depending on where you are in business.

It doesn't matter if you have the most booming business in the world; every business needs to have a goal, PERIOD. Having and setting a goal in your business is key to more and more success. Every time you accomplish your goal, you are pushing your business further and further into more success. Even if you do not reach your goal every time, it is important that you have a goal.

When setting your weekly goal, it is important to think about:

- How much product you will be selling weekly
- How to make your goal to be realistic
  - Base your goal around how you are already selling. If you are already selling 5 of your products a week, then you would want to sell at least 8-10 of your products.
- How you are going to attract your customers
- Ask yourself how you are going to market your products to reach your goal – social media, emails, etc.
- What day and time are you going to reset your goal?

Having a goal will help the growth of your business. When trying to secure a bag, you should leverage your goal to help grow your clientele and reach out to new customers.

<u>Bag Talk Notes</u>

BAG TIP #21

BAG TIP #21 is keeping a positive mindset and ignoring the haters, PERIOD. When you first start your business, you will be discouraged. But you need to understand that everything will be ok. It is important to be aware that there will be times in business where your clientele just gets dry. But the key is to realize that you have to STAY POSITIVE AND KEEP PUSHING. You may never know how close you are to securing the biggest bag ever, so it is important that you keep pushing.

It is also important that you stay away from negative people and negative energy. When I started my business, I made sure that I distanced myself from people who were going to distract me from my business, guide me onto the wrong path, and also discourage me from completing my goals. So it is important to have some real people behind you that support you.

Having a business can be a little overwhelming, especially if you have another job, or If you are in school. It is important to take small day breaks to keep a clean and positive mindset. For example, here are a few things you can to do clear your mind:

- Read a book
    - Reading books that pertain to increasing your business would help you stay motivated and focused throughout your business journey.
- Workout
    - I am personally into fitness, so sometimes when I am stressed out, I like to knock out a good body pump class.
- Read motivational quotes
- Watch motivational videos
    - Now when I am STRESSED OUT, I like to watch a few motivational videos on YouTube, especially on Instagram. My favorite motivational speakers' Instagram accounts are @coachstormy and @garyvee

<u>Bag Talk Notes</u>

_____

_____

_____

_____

_____

_____

_____

_____

_____

_____

Conclusion

Look at you now! You finished the 21 tips, and now you're in route to securing your bag! Though this is just a book to get you started, it is important to come back and read over things after you started your business just to make sure that everything is going well at the early stages of your business journey. I think it is amazing that you decided to start your own business and hopefully, it will inspire the people you know to start their business as well. During your business journey, I want you to have the same positive mindset. Also, I want you to remember never to give up because you never know how close you are to securing the bag of your dreams.

Contact Information

website: www.soglossy.me
Instagram: @soglossy.me
@youlovearica_

Interested in Writing and Publishing a Book
Visit us @www.a2zbookspublishing.net

www.ingramcontent.com/pod-product-compliance
Lightning Source LLC
Chambersburg PA
CBHW071459210326
41597CB00018B/2608